ŠEVČÍK
Op. 1 Parts 3 & 4

SCHOOL OF TECHNIQUE

SCHULE DER TECHNIK

ÉCOLE DE TECHNIQUE

for

VIOLA

(ALTO)

arranged / bearbeitet / arrangées

by   von   par

Lionel Tertis

Italian viola by Pietro Giovanni Mantegazza, c. 1780,
with kind permission of Christie's, London.

Bosworth

REMEMBER!

(1) The first consideration in string playing, is the attainment of *perfect intonation*. This can only be achieved by the most *intense* and *concentrated* listening, (not superficial listening). *Never* pass a note that is the slightest degree out of tune.

(2) *Hold* and *keep* your fingers down on the strings in all these exercises, whenever and wherever it is at all possible.

(3) Attention must be paid to accurate note *values*. Be particularly careful when there are two notes with *separate* bows, immediately followed by two notes of the same value in one bow, or one note separately, followed by three notes of the same value in one bow etc. etc. No matter how varied the groupings, every note must be of exact equal value.

(4) When practising these exercises *slowly* lift your fingers high and feel you are doing so from the *knuckles* and bring your fingers down hard on the fingerboard,—when practising them *rapidly,* do not lift your fingers high and put them down *lightly* on the fingerboard.

(5) Divide the bowing up so as to, *first,* practise the exercises slowly and play them in tune. When you can do this efficiently, use the bowing as indicated, or as many notes in the one bow as possible.

NOTICE

(1) La première qualité qu'il faut s'appliquer à obtenir, lors de l'étude de tout instrument à cordes, est la *justesse d'intonation.* Celle-ci ne s'acquiert qu'au prix d'une attention *soutenue* et *concentrée* (pas d'attention superficielle). Veillez donc à ce que chaque note soit rigoureusement juste sans faire la plus minime concession à la médiocrité.

(2) Au cours de ces exercices *posez* et *maintenez* les doigts bien appuyes sur les cordes partout où la chose est possible.

(3) Observez minutieusement la *valeur* des notes. Veillez y specialement lorsque deux notes avec coups d'archet *séparés* se trouvent être suivies de deux autres notes de même valeur mais figurant dans un même coup d'archet, ou lorsqu'une note isolée est suivie de trois notes de même valeur dans un même coup d'archet, etc.. Les diverses façons dont les notes peuvent être groupées importent peu, pourvu qu'à chacune d'elles il soit toujours donné sa valeur adéquate.

(4) Commencez par jouer ces exercices *au ralenti* et faites en sorte que les doigts s'élèvent très haut. Il faut vraiment sentir que tout le travail se fait dans les charnières des *articulations.* Abaissez ensuite avec force les doigts sur le manche. Lorsque, par la suite, vous jouez ces exercices en un tempo plus *accéléré,* levez les doigts moins haut et abaissez les sur le manche avec plus de légèreté.

(5) Répartissez vos coups d'archet de manière à jouer d'abord ces exercices en un tempo assez lent mais toujours avec une intonation rigoureusement juste. Dès que vous serez à même de jouer de la sorte avec aisance, accélérez et conformez-vous aux indications des coups d'archet tout en vous appliquant à jouer le plus de notes possibles en un seul coup d'archet.

ZUR BEACHTUNG

(1) Von vordringlicher Wichtigkeit für das Spielen auf Streichinstrumenten ist *untadelig-saubere Intonation.* Diese kann nur erreicht werden durch intensiv-konzentriertes (niemals oberflächliches) *Hören.* Lass keinen Ton durchgehen, der auch nur im geringsten unrein in der Stimmung ist.

(2) Lass bei diesen Übungen die *Finger auf der Saite liegen,* soweit und solange es möglich ist.

(3) Achte auf genaue *Notenwerte,* besonders wenn auf zwei *einzeln gestrichene* Noten unmittelbar zwei *gebundene* Noten gleichen Wertes folgen — oder auf eine einzeln gestrichene Note drei gebundene gleichen Wertes usw. Ganz gleichgültig, wie die Notengruppen auf den Bogen verteilt sind: Stets muss jede Note genau den ihr zugehörigen Wert erhalten.

(4) Beim *langsamen* Üben die Finger hoch (aus dem Knöchelgelenk) aufheben und energisch auf das Griffbrett aufsetzen—beim *schnellen* Üben nur wenig aufheben und locker aufsetzen.

(5) Studiere die Übungen *zuerst langsam* mit sauberer, schöner Tongebung, dann erst halte dich an die angegebenen Bögen oder spiele auf einen Bogen so viel Noten wie möglich.

B. & Co. Ltd. 21508c

SEVCIK. Op. 1 — Viola (Alto)

TROISIÈME PARTIE
Changement des Positions

Changez de position sans saccades.
On travaillera chaque exercice
Legato et une note par coup d'archet.

THIRD PART
Changes of Position

Change positions without jerks.
Practise each exercise. Legato and
also one note to a bow.

DRITTER TEIL
Lagenwechsel

Lagenwechsel ohne jeden Ruck.
Man übe jedes Beispiel. Jede Note
einzeln gestrichen wie auch mit den
angegebenen legato = Bögen zu üben.

1

Gammes sur une corde | *Scales on one string* | *Tonleitern auf einer Saite*

Copyright MCMLIII by Bosworth & Co. Ltd.

21508c

2

Gammes en trois octaves | *Scales over three octaves* | *Tonleitern durch drei Oktaven*

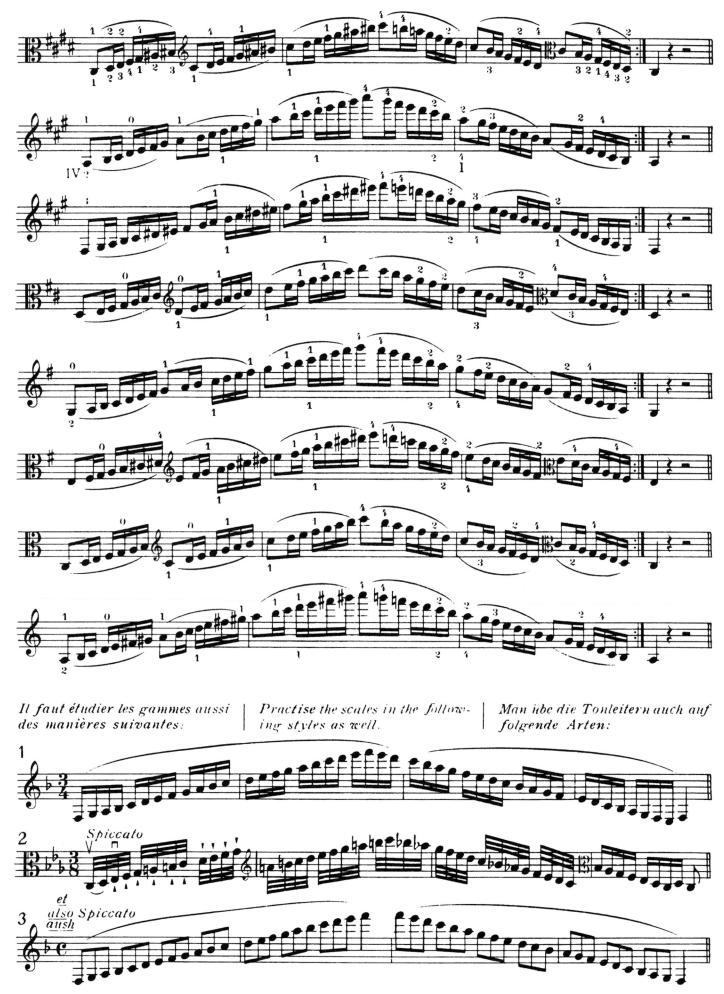

Il faut étudier les gammes aussi des manières suivantes: | Practise the scales in the following styles as well. | Man übe die Tonleitern auch auf folgende Arten:

3

Arpèges sur une corde. | Arpeggios on one string. | Arpeggien auf einer Saite.

4

Arpèges en trois octaves | Arpeggios over three octaves | Arpeggien durch drei Oktaven

5

14

6

Pour mémoire: l'intonation à vérifier! | *To remind! Intonation!* | *Achte auf die Intonation!*

B. & Co. 21508c

7

8

Gamme chromatique | The Chromatic Scale | Chromatische Tonleiter

9

B.& Co. Ltd 21508c

10

Changez les positions en glissades légères, évitez les saccades autant que possible.

Change positions with discreet portamento, avoid jerks as much as possible.

Wechsle die Lagen durch leichtes Hinübergleiten, Sprünge möglichst vermeiden.

B.& Co.Ltd. 21508c

B. & Co. Ltd. 21508c

11

12

Cet exercice doit être exécuté aussi sur la 2me, 3me et 4me corde.

This exercise must also be practiced on the 2nd, 3rd and 4th strings.

Diese Übung ist auch auf der 2ten 3ten und 4ten Saite auszuführen.

QUATRIÈME PARTIE
Exercices en doubles cordes

FOURTH PART
Exercises in Double Stopping

VIERTER TEIL
Übungen in Doppelgriffen

1

Octaves | *Octaves* | *Oktaven*

Jouez lentement pour commencer. Un coup d'archet par noire.

Practise slowly first— one bow to each crotchet.

Zunächst langsam üben— für jede Viertelnote einen Bogen.

3

4

Tierces	*Thirds*	*Terzen*
L'intonation! Changements de position nets et sans exagération dans le portamento.	Intonation! Clean changes of position without overdone portamento.	Intonation! Sauberer Lagenwechsel ohne großes portamento.

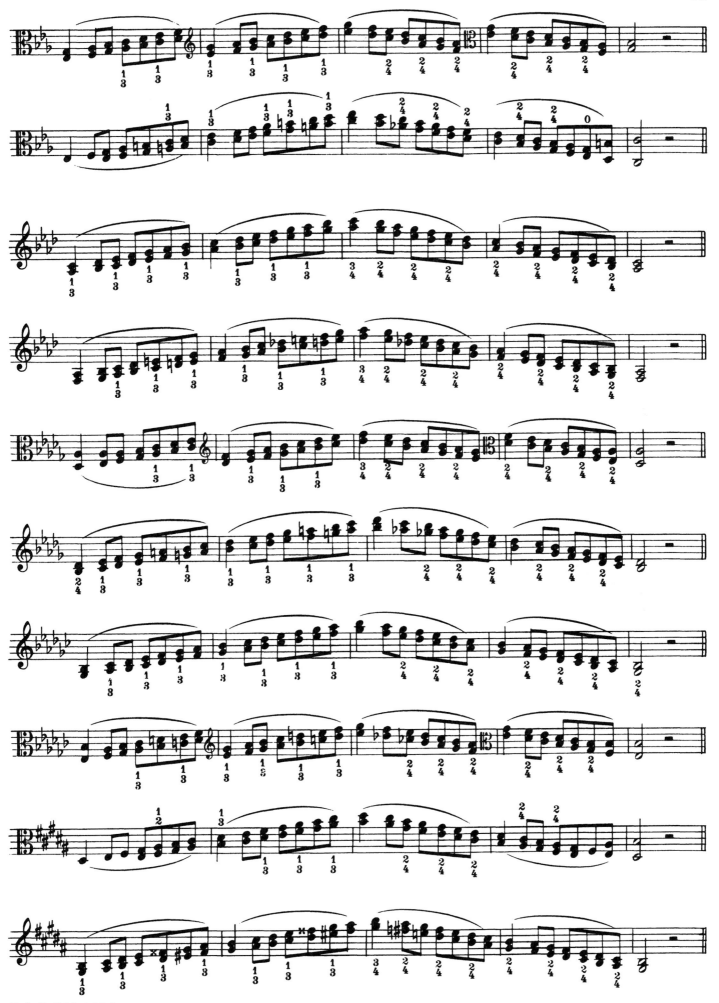

5

Sixtes | Sixths | Sexten

7

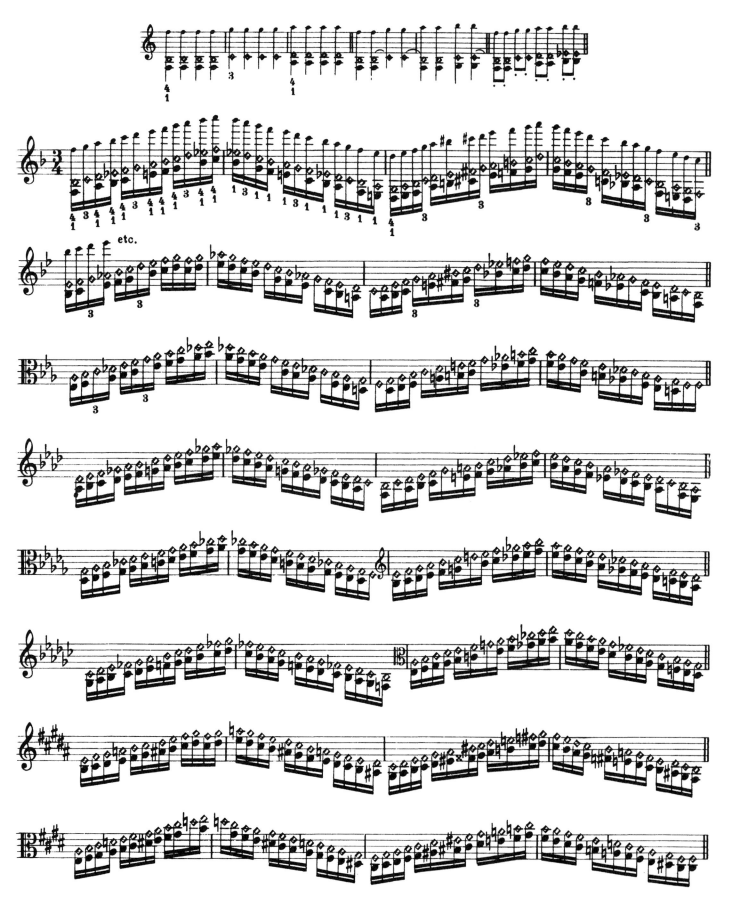

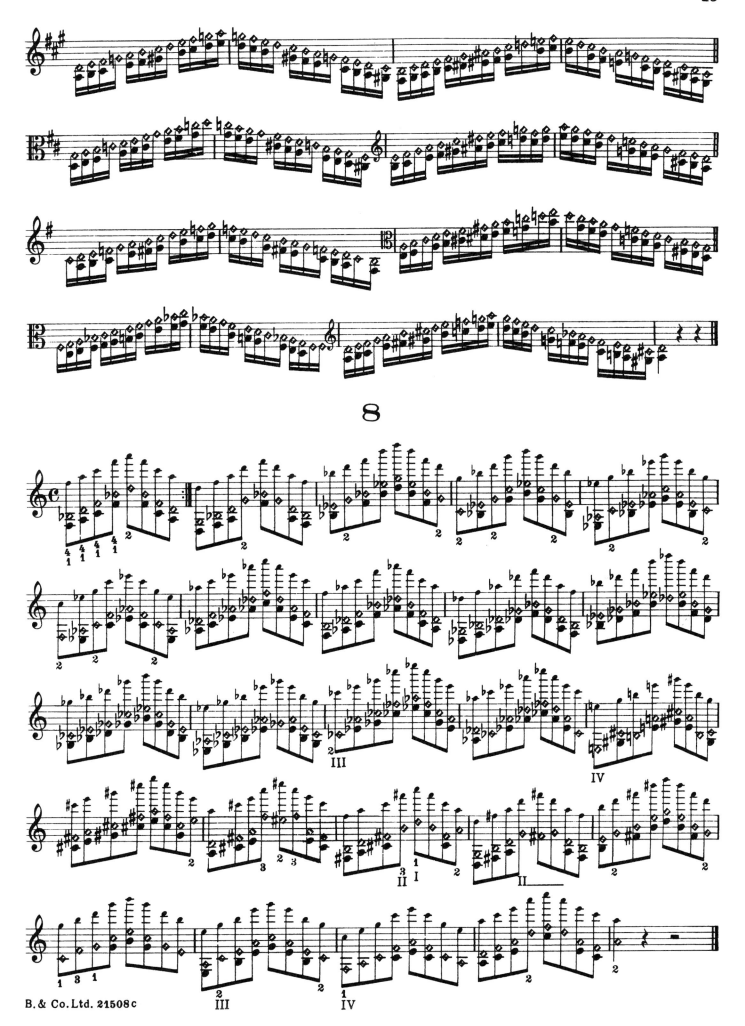

8

PUBLISHERS OF MUSIC FOR THE SERIOUS VIOLIST

Studies

ARNOLD, Alan
3-Octave Scales & Arpeggios
BLUMENSTENGAL, A.
Viola Scale Technique Bk.1 - 1st Pos.
Viola Scale Technique Bk.2 -1-5 Pos.
HOFMANN, Richard
Melodic Double-Stop Studies Op. 96
TARTINI, Giuseppe
The Art of Bowing

Viola Solo

ARNOLD, Alan
Cadenzas for Telemann Viola Concerto
KREISLER, Fritz
Recitative and Scherzo Caprice
WOEHR, Christian
Bachiana

Viola & Piano Albums

ARNOLD, Alan
The Young Violist Bk. 1 (easy pieces)
The Young Violist Bk. 2 (more pieces)
BACH, J.S.
Basic Bach (arr.Arnold)
BEETHOVEN, Ludwig van
Beethoven's Best (arr. Arnold)
MOZART, W.A
Mozart Miniatures (arr. Arnold)

Viola & Piano Repertoire

BACH, J.S.
Bourrée in C minor
Chromatic Fantasy and Fugue
BEETHOVEN, Ludwig van
Für Elise
BENJAMIN, Arthur
Jamaican Rumba
BOCCHERINI, Luigi
Music Box Minuet
BÖHM, Carl
Sarabande
BOROWSKI, Felix
Adoration
BRAHMS, Johannes
Scherzo
CHOPIN, Frédéric
Nocturne
CORELLI, Arcangelo
Sarabande, Giga and Badinerie
Sonata No.12 - La Folia con
Variazione

DANCLA, Charles
Carnival of Venice
DE BÉRIOT, Ch.
Scène de Ballet
DEBUSSY, Claude
Girl with the Flaxen Hair
La Plus Que Lente
DVORÁK, Antonin
Romance Op. 11
Sonatina Op. 100
FAURÉ, Gabriel
Fantasie
FIOCCO, Gioseffo-Hectore
Allegro
FRANCOEUR, François
Sonata in A
GLUCK, Christoff W. von
Melody from *Orfeo ed Euridice*
HANDEL, G.F.
Bourrée
Concerto in B flat
Sonata in B flat
Sonata in D
HUBAY, Jenö
Hejre Kati
JENKINSON, Ezra
Elves' Dance (*Elfentanz*)
JOPLIN, Scott
Pineapple Rag
Solace
KREISLER, Fritz
Liebesfreud
Liebesleid
Praeludium and Allegro
Sicilienne and Rigaudon
MASSENET, Jules
Meditation from *Thaïs*
MATTHEWS, Holon
Fantasy
MENDELSSOHN, Felix
Sonata in E flat
MOZART, W.A.
Adagio K.261
Menuetto Divertimento K.334
Rondo K.250
Serenata Cantabile
MUSSORGSKY, Modest
Hopak
NOVACEK, Ottokar
Perpetual Motion
PAGANINI, Niccolò
Six Sonatas Bk. 1, Nos 1, 2,3
Six Sonatas Bk. 2, Nos 4, 5, 6
Variations on the G-String
PUGNANI, Gaetano
Gavotta Variata

RACHMANINOFF, Sergei
Vocalise
RIES, Franz
Perpetuum Mobile
RIMSKY-KORSAKOV, N.
Flight of the Bumble Bee
SCHMIDT, Ernst
Alla Turca
SHUBERT, Franz
The Bee
TARTINI, Giuseppe
Sonata angelique
The Devil's Trill
TCHAIKOVSKY, P.
Canzonetta
June Barcarolle
Mélodie
Sérénade mélancholique
Valse sentimentale
VITALI, Giovanni
Chaconne
VIVALDI, Antonio
Sonata in G
WEBER, Carl M.
Andante and Hungarian Rondo
WIENIAWSKI, Henryk
Légende
Scherzo Tarantella

Viola Duos

BACH, J. S.
Fifteen Two-Part Inventions
MOZART, W.A.
Duo Sonata in B flat K.292
Twelve Duets K.487

3 Violas & Piano

PACHELBEL, Johann
Canon

4 Violas

TELEMANN, Georg Philipp
Concerto No. 1 in C for 4 Violas
Concerto No. 2 in G for 4 Violas
Concerto No. 3 in F for 4 Violas
Concerto No. 4 in D for 4 Violas

4 Violas & Piano

VIVALDI, Antonio
Concerto for 4 Violas and Piano

Available from:

Bosworth